Rocks Across the Pond
Lessons Learned. Stories Told.

Our son Justin was just ten years old when Kathy and I had our first glimpse of things to come. As fathers and sons have done from time eternal, Justin and I were skipping rocks across a pond near our home when I decided to heave one as far as I could to impress my little ballplayer. To my astonishment, after watching my attempt splash about halfway across, little Justin picked up a rock and launched it all the way into the trees on the other side. Little did we know that this was just the first of what would fondly come to be known as "pinch me moments." There were many more to come as we began our incredible journey with our boys and baseball.

It is a story we want to share....

Richard and Kathy Verlander
Recipients of the
George and Barbara Bush
Little League Parents of the Year Award

Stephen M. Watson, Editor

Wayne Dementi
Publisher
Dementi Milestone Publishing

First Printing

Authors
Richard and Kathy Verlander

Publisher
Wayne Dementi
Dementi Milestone Publishing, Inc.
Manakin-Sabot, VA 23103
www.dementimilestonepublishing.com

Cataloging-in-publication data for this book is available from
The Library of Congress.
ISBN: 978-0-9850375-0-5

Graphic design by:
Jayne E. Hushen

Research and editorial support by:
Stephen M. Watson

Printed in the USA

Cover image: Dallas Bolster, of Dundee, Michigan, gets a fist-pump from Detroit Tigers starting pitcher, Justin Verlander, before a game against the Los Angeles Angels, Sunday, July 31, 2011 in Detroit. AP Photo by Duane Burleson.

The Bolster family are avid Detroit Tigers fans. The rest of Dallas's family includes (l. to r.) Renee, with son Daniel laying on the deck. Then, Drew is behind him. Dallas is behind Drew. Sitting on the deck is the oldest son, Derrick. Dan, is kneeling in the back. *Bolster Family photo.*

Dedication

This book is dedicated to the grandparents - Minton B. Ryder, Olympia Ryder, Richard C. Verlander, Sr. and Margaret Verlander. Being great parents is a gift that perpetuates itself generation after generation. The greatest tribute we can offer to their legacy is to pay it forward.

Kathy and Richard Verlander

TABLE OF CONTENTS

Acknowledgements

In 2010, we began this book with a vision of sharing, and celebrating, the complimentary values associated with parenting, family values and baseball. That concept has been our mantra throughout our journey. We have been affirmed along the way with so many people who delighted in our goal. We wish to acknowledge them now.

We believe you will thoroughly enjoy the photography that you will see throughout our book. We have been blessed with so much assistance from so many companies and organizations, who have made their wonderful files available to us. Our special appreciation goes to The Detroit News, Major League Baseball, Getty Images, AP World Wide Images, Fox Sports News, the Detroit Tigers, the Goochland Gazette and the Verlander Family.

To Jayne Hushen, who assisted us with the presentation of the material, we say "Thank you very much." Many individuals provided us with stories and research help. Our appreciation is extended to FoxSports writer, Dana Wakiji and her husband, Tom Gromak. Justin's coaches offered invaluable insights for us. To wit: Bob Smith (AAU), Bryan Gordon (Goochland High School) and Tony Guzzo (Old Dominion University). Justin's childhood friend, Daniel Hicks, offered stories that only a childhood friend could offer. A special moment for the book team happened upon a visit to Mrs. Marion Kramer's 3rd Grade Class, where we became even more aware of how youngsters think as they grow and develop.

Many people have guided us in our quest to do justice to our theme. Thanks to Justin's agents, Mike Milchin and Jeff Feinstein, for their support.

Others whose contributions have meant so much to us include Kelly Breckenridge, Manager of the Detroit Shoppe, Todd "Parney" Parnell, General Manager of the Richmond Flying Squirrels Baseball Team, Jay Shively of the Goochland County YMCA, Chris Finwood, head coach Old Dominion University, Julie, Will and Katie Watson, Dianne Dementi, Hart Dementi, Austin Warner and the Verlanders' "footwarmers" Curtis, Riley and Miss B.

A number of organizations have rallied to our side, including the Tuckahoe Little League, the Detroit Tigers, Major League Baseball, Comerica Park ushers and attendants.

Lastly, our appreciation is extended to a number of others whose behind-the-scenes support was invaluable. Thank you Patsy Arnett, Aynsley Fisher, Fletcher Watson, Mary Jo Shea, Carrell Blanton Garrett & Van Horn, PLC, and Stephen Frey.

A Special Salute

THE DETROIT NEWS

It has been our experience that The Detroit News is committed to improving the greater Detroit community. The Detroit News' team of photographers capture unparalleled images that celebrate Detroit ~ its people, its spirit and its sense of community. We are proud to share these wonderful images with you.

THANK YOU DETROIT NEWS

2006 World Series

I've been here before...

Walking in the shadows of Comerica Park in downtown Detroit, Kathy and I braced ourselves against the cold, raw wind, with Ben in tow close behind.

They call baseball players "the boys of summer," but the weather conditions more suited a hockey match. I hitched the collar of my coat up further on my neck as we entered through the main gate and showed the attendant our tickets.

He looked at our tickets, smiled pleasantly, and then "shot" the tickets with his hand-held laser gun and waved us on.

The load-bearing concrete supports and painted steel girders were so much colder and more menacing than they appeared in the summer, but the banners, and bustling of all the fans packing into the park kept us company as we moved to the seats that Justin had provided for this special game.

I thought back to our seats the first time we came to Comerica Park to watch Justin play. We were so new at this—and so was Justin. None of us knew, or even thought to ask, if parents got special seats for home games. As a consequence, when we presented our tickets to the attendant, we got a different kind of smile.

"Go up to the right, then go up some more stairs, and then go up some more," he said with a chuckle. We ended up in the high nosebleed section, further up than Bob Uecker—"He missed the tag! He missed the tag!"

When the fans around us found out that we were one of the player's parents, they started laughing too. It seems a lot of people found us funny back in those days, and well, we were so new at this that I guess we were really rather silly. But it sure was fun.

But now this. This was the big time. The first game of the 2006 World Series between our Detroit Tigers and the St. Louis Cardinals.

As we settled into our seats behind home plate, I thought back about what a year it had been. The anticipation and ultimate joy of celebrating Justin making the 25-player roster out of spring training, to now watching him pitch to start Game One of the World Series. What a whirlwind!

Kathy wrapped the blanket around us and we huddled up to try to stave off the bitter cold.

I found myself taking in the moment, my eyes surveying Comerica Park from our vantage point. It all looked so different, so festive. There were banners draped from the bleachers and American flags popping up everywhere. There was electricity in the air that can come from only a big event like the World Series. Even the loudspeaker sounded more regal—and loud!

They had begun the introductions of the starting lineups.

..."and warming up in the bullpen, starting pitcher, Justin Verlander!"

Everyone turned toward the bullpen and the gate opened up. There, warming up, with the unmistakable high back leg kick silhouetted against the backdrop, was Justin. The roar of the crowd reached a crescendo and then he and the pitching coach walked out onto the field. Everything seemed to move in slow motion.

I was so very aware of the moment and trying to take it all in—to absorb what so many great players never got to experience—the World Series, the pinnacle of this professional sport.

I felt a chill that was due to much more than the weather. Turning to look at Kathy and Ben, I could tell that they felt it too. This was a moment our family will be talking about for generations to come.

I look back to the field and watch Justin walk toward the mound, and yep, there's the hop and jump across the foul line that we had gotten so accustomed to seeing since his teenage years. I'm watching Justin, listening to the roar of the crowd, and feeling the excitement.

And then a strange calm comes over me... My mind is telling me to relax. I've been here before, it says. But how can that be...?

I'm back in 1995 and it's a beautiful warm summer evening. Butterflies scatter from the outfield as our Phillies Majors team takes the field to take on the heralded "A's" from the American League. It's the biggest event of the year, The Tuckahoe Little League Twelve and under Championship game!

WHOOOSH!

A dusty baseball whizzes by and just misses the rim of my Phillies baseball cap as I stand by the dugout, surely a sign that Justin was "getting loose" in the bullpen.

"Okay, son," I say, turning to Justin, "head on out to the field and take a few warm-ups from the mound."

I watched as he tugged down his cap and headed out to the field, taking a small leap over the foul line as he made his way to the mound. His confident stride only reminded me of how nervous I was.

As head coach I was so proud of the team and felt that we were ready for the battle, but I still had the pregame jitters. It was as if the butterflies that had been fluttering around the outfield had all flitted into my stomach.

"Batter up!" yelled the umpire behind the plate.

I look out at my son, standing tall and determined on the mound. I watched him wind up, rear back, and fire a strike to...

...David Eckstein, lead-off batter for the St. Louis Cardinals.

I was back in the cold stands of Comerica Park in Detroit and the 2006 World Series was underway. Boy, what a feeling! Yet, it was a feeling I had experienced before—on a smaller scale, perhaps, but it was the same feeling, and the same adrenaline rush.

And man, this was fun.

What a ride!

TIGERS

ComericA
PARK

ORIOLES

11	Andino	2B	.266
*2	Hardy	SS	.266
21	Markakis	RF	.282
27	Guerrero	DH	.292
32	Wieters	C	
10	Jones	CF	.263
12	Reynolds	1B	.224
19	Davis	3B	.260
14	Reimold	LF	.241

| 48 | Porcello | P | 4.79 |

2 Hardy   SS
AVG   R   H   HR   RBI
.266   73   13   29   76
OB%   SLG   S. FLY
.306   48   5

1st-
SINGLED TO RIGHT-CENTER

BALL	STRIKE	OUT
1	1	0

	1	2	3	4	5	6	7	8	9		H	E	
ORIOLES	1	0											7:44 PM
TIGERS	2	0											58°F

Firestone

BELLE
TIRE

Leading
Michigan
to a
healthier
future

Blue Cross Blue Shield
bcbsm.com

Orio
2

xfinity®
Comcast

xfinity   Porcello   91   15   57   42

UNDER ARMOUR   Dunham's
SPORTS
www.dunhamssports.com

pepsi

UHY Certified Public Accountants   UHY Certified Public Accountants

CHOOSE TASTE   BIC

Wait Times at DMC.org

Fields of Dreams

*"May the good Lord be with you down every road you roam,
and may sunshine and happiness surround you when you're far from home"*

Rod Stewart, Bob Dylan, Jim Cregan, Kevin Savigar

O ur belief has always been that it is our responsibility to encourage our boys to reach for their dreams, both professionally, and spiritually. After all, reaching for a dream requires a plan, and without a plan, a dream is just a fantasy. In pursuit of the dream, whatever it might be, we have also stressed the importance of happiness and significance over substance. In other words, if achieving your dreams doesn't make you a better person, then you will be left feeling unfulfilled, no matter how many records you set, how much money you make, or how many followers you have.

None of us ever knows where the pursuit of a dream may lead us, or how divergent the path may become, but almost universally we all regret never having tried.

Upon reflection, we realize that the real dream for us is to be blessed to play an important role in our children's journey.

Where it all began - Justin (center) at Tuckahoe
Little League T-Ball Field, Richmond, VA, 1989.

Richard on "The Hill" at Tuckahoe Little League National Field.

Tuckahoe Li

RICHMO

Richard Verlander, coach of 1995 Champion Phillies,
Tuckahoe Little League.

League Field

IRGINIA

3

Goochland County High School
2001 Results

72 Innings Pitched
144 Strike-outs
0.29 Earned Run Average

Old Dominion University, Norfolk, VA,
college home for Justin and Ben Verlander.
Justin earned All America honors, was selected for Team USA, and
became the all-time career strikeout leader for ODU, the Colonial
Athletic Conference, and the State of Virginia in just 3 years.

5

Justin began his pro
Lakeland Tigers o

onal career with The
rida State League.

Walt Whitman once said, "I see great things in Baseball. It's our game, the American game. It will repair our losses and be a blessing to us."

-- *Annie Savoy*
Bull Durham 1988

The Show

Justin's Major League debut came on July 5, 2005 as part of a day/night double-header against the Cleveland Indians. We had gotten "the call" just a few days earlier.

Like other moments that come upon us suddenly and are of such significance as to leave an indelible mark on the rest of our lives, I was transfixed in the moment. I will never forget the exact spot I was standing in our garage in Goochland, Virginia on that hot sunny day when we first got the big news.

A few short days later and we were in downtown Cleveland, hours before the Tigers second game of the day with Justin as a big league starter!

While Justin went to the field early (as usual), Kathy, Ben, and I found ourselves with a few hours to spend before the game. To calm my nerves, I decided to walk from the team hotel to the Rock and Roll Hall of Fame. Having played guitar in a band myself, it was easy to get lost in the nostalgia of the 60's and 70's artists and music, and before I knew it, it was time to head for the ballpark.

teams were warming up out on the field. "Geez," I thought to myself, "the Cleveland Indians are the hottest team in baseball right now. Couldn't we have arranged an easier opponent for Justin's debut?"

Having found our seats, (which I of course had NO CHANCE of actually remaining in) I wandered (paced) over to the bullpen to watch Justin warm up. Looking down in the pen along with quite a few fans, I saw Justin getting ready.

Pop!

The sound of Justin's fastball slapping into the mitt of the catcher. It was a sound I had heard thousands of times before, but it was never quite like this. It was all so much grander now, the scale expanding beyond the comprehension of my senses of sight and sound. It was all so surreal to me. My heart was in my throat and tears filled my eyes. This was it…our son in the BIG LEAGUES.

To experience Justin walking out to the mound that night in Cleveland was a dream come true. He struggled a bit and took the loss, but left everyone impressed with his poise and raw ability. As the skipper pulled him from the game and he walked back to the dugout, Justin gave a fleeting glimpse back to the field. While this was only a spot start and one of two big league appearances in 2005, it was clear that he belonged.

I am just so thrilled that the whole family was able to be a part of this milestone in Justin's life, and I know that none of us will ever forget it.

***

Parents are the Key

The most precious gift we have to offer our young athlete with big dreams is our time.

Richard Verlander

The single most important element for raising successful young athletes is to stay involved in their lives. Get involved in your young athletes life. Make the time to be there, and watch them grow!

Whether you are the biological parent or adoptive, an older brother or sister, or maybe just a caring mentor, kids need someone to look for in the stands.

Did you ever notice who the first person your youngster looks for is when he gets a hit? Or a strikeout???

It often goes unnoticed, but as a coach in Little League I sometimes wondered if parents know just how much our sons and daughters want to please us and how important our approval is in their young lives.

Is there a connection here? When we look back we see similar trends off the baseball field. High achieving students also seem to have adult role models that are actively engaged in and supporting their children's education. While attending parent teacher conferences, or when serving as volunteers at other school functions, we have noticed parental involvement as it equates with success in the classroom. Conversely, we have heard teachers often lament the fact that the students that are most in need of help often do not have a parent at the meeting.

Parents at Godwin

Justin attended and played baseball and basketball (his "fun sport") at Goochland High School. Goochland is the next county just west of Henrico County, Virginia, abutting each other on the north side of the James River. When Justin was about 6 years old, Kathy and I lived in Henrico County, and that is where we were introduced to Tuckahoe Little League. Justin started out with T-ball, and played for many years, even after we had moved out of Henrico and into Goochland County. As the rule goes, as long as the father is a coach, the son can play for Tuckahoe Little League, even if living in a different county.

Having spent so much time with the boys and their fathers from Henrico County, it was only natural that I would take an interest in the boys' baseball careers. Many of the boys that played at Tuckahoe Little League went on to play at Godwin High School in Henrico County. Rightfully so, Godwin was, and still is, admired as a baseball powerhouse. In fact, in 1999, Justin's sophomore year of High School, Godwin won the District, Regional and State Championships.

I loved to go over and watch the young men that I had gotten to know so well during my years of coaching Tuckahoe Little League. It was fun following their progress, and I have to admit that it is still fun to keep up with them and see what they are doing. It's been a thrill watching these kids go off to colleges like Notre Dame, the University of Virginia, Virginia Tech, and the University of Richmond. There's a Harvard Law School graduate, a Johns Hopkins Medical School student, successful businessmen, and yes, a Major Leaguer.

One day, as I hung over the fence watching a Godwin game,

Team mom Kathy Verlander prepares a T-Baller to bat.

12

one of the other fathers struck up a conversation. He seemed mildly intrigued that I was at Godwin watching the game even though my son didn't go there, but reminding him of my experience with the kids through Tuckahoe Little League seemed to satisfy him pretty quickly.

"You know," he said, nodding toward the Godwin players out on the field, "I guess you're right. A lot of those kids did play at Tuckahoe Little League."

"Yep," I agreed.

"But you know what else?" he said, turning toward the stands, and making sure that my eye followed his, "take a good look at the people in those stands. The kids on that field are the ones who have his parents in those stands."

Richard (standing) listens as coach Rocky Moorefield gives instructions to 9 year old Cardinals Tuckahoe Little League 1992.

He turned and faced me directly now. "And those are the same parents that were at the practices and games at Tuckahoe Little League, and most of them were coaches or team moms."

It took me a second, but I got what he was saying. The kids on that field had the parents that stayed involved. There were plenty of really good ballplayers at Tuckahoe Little League, but there were a considerable number of them that didn't get the family support. And my friend at Godwin that evening was right. Those kids weren't in the game anymore.

Mom Kathy Verlander is on the edge of her seat as little brother plays in the dirt (left).

14

Talent vs. Skill

Justin Verlander is a natural, he's gifted, electric arm, very fast, smart, has power, quick feet... he has all the tools! What a talent!

Or ...

Look at that Ben Verlander's swing! He stays inside the ball, has great mechanics, and is short to the ball. And when he gets on base he gets such good jumps he's always a threat to steal!

What's the difference?

Well, the difference is, your young athlete can be a great baseball player with talent, or skill, or both. But not either.

Huh???

Let me explain the good news.

As a baseball parent, over the years I have seen many young people with tremendous talent that have never made it to their full potential, because they lacked the skills needed to play baseball at a high level. Baseball is a skill game and you cannot play it without learning good technique. You simply will not play the game well without good skills, no matter how talented you are.

Justin shows "The Glare" at an early age.

So what's the good news?

Unlike many sports, baseball is a game that can be played at the very highest level through hard work, determination, and grit. You don't have to be the biggest, fastest, or tallest. Just look at the Major League ball players. You have all shapes and sizes, big and strong, short and stout, fast and slow. The one thing they all have in common is skill!

Skills can be learned. Talent can't. That's the difference. But to be a good baseball player, unlike many sports, you can overcome a lack of natural ability through good instruction and HARD WORK, HARD WORK, HARD WORK!!!!

Did I mention HARD WORK????

I might not be fast, but I get great jumps and take good routes to the ball...

I might not be quick, but I am a savvy base runner...

I might not have a great arm, but I get rid of the ball fast and have good footwork, so I always make accurate throws...

I don't hit a lot of home runs, but I almost always make contact and I learned how to hit to the opposite field so I drive in a lot of runs...

I don't throw hard, but I throw strikes and seldom walk people...

and on and on...

Here is an interesting point. It has been my observation that young athletes develop at very different times as their bodies mature. Boys especially seem to reach puberty and become more man-like in their physical makeup at different ages. So if your youngster learns the skills to play the game right now, then as he gets bigger, stronger and faster, perhaps later than some of his peers, he will be prepared to best utilize his suddenly acquired talents. When skill meets talent you have, well... Justin Verlander.

Justin was 6'2" and weighed 170 lbs. when he went to college at Old Dominion University with a 92 MPH fastball. In spite of countless hours of hard work honing his skills, and earning a scholarship to play college baseball, he went undrafted out of high school. By the time he was a junior, three years later, he was 6'5" and weighed a strapping 215 lbs. with a 98 mph fastball. He was drafted 2nd overall in the first round in the Major League Baseball draft by the Detroit Tigers. Years of hard work, both on the field, as well as in the gym and in the classroom converged with his late bloomer physique.

Today we just smile when people say it comes so easy for Justin—he's a "natural."

Justin (top), and brother Ben (right), worked hard to hone their skills.

Control

Self-control is the quality that distinguishes the fittest to surive.
-- George Bernard Shaw

Young baseball players, especially pitchers, often struggle with control. Usually this can be corrected by learning proper mechanics and not overthrowing. Proper technique will not only help to develop more consistency in the strike zone, but will also help young arms stay healthy. Many of the all-time great pitchers, including Justin's hero, Nolan Ryan, battled to harness their raw ability and channel their energy and focus early in their careers. Justin was no different and has worked hard to become a "pitcher" and not just a "thrower." He was rewarded in 2007 when he hurled his first no-hitter and got a congratulatory call from—you guessed it—Nolan Ryan!

But controlling the baseball is the easy part. We have coaches, how-to books, and drills to hone our skills. But parents know only too well that there is another kind of "control" that is not so easy to address. When little Johnny strikes out, or misses the pop fly, we far too often see little Johnny lose his temper. He loses his cool. He loses control. Losing control in this sense can be far more detrimental to the kid's development than controlling balls and strikes.

As the parents of budding athletes, we believe that our role in teaching kids to control themselves is much more involved. We must instill the notion that control, simply stated, is self-discipline. We have always believed that self-discipline is one of the greatest lessons we can teach as our boys strive to become high achievers in sports, and in life. Viewed in the context of reaching goals and realizing dreams, "control" becomes a vital tool. Sadly, many athletes that Justin grew up with never realized their dream because while they had great talent they never possessed the control/self-discipline needed to climb the ladder of success and beat the competition in a very tough game.

So what can my youngster control that makes such a difference?

As I said before, there are resources that will help us learn physical control. Coaches can instruct us, and how-to books overflow the shelves in the bookstores. But are there resources and tools that we can turn to help with the self-control? Absolutely!

Work ethic- can you outwork your competition?

Good Grades- can I study harder? Will I qualify for a college scholarship?

Fitness- will you be at your best if you are in poor physical condition?

Nutrition- do you eat a healthy diet?

Rest…young people need 8-10 hours a night minimum to be at maximum performance on the field and in the classroom. How late are you up playing video games?

Justin teaches younger brother, Ben, control.

Attitude…can you control your attitude and respect others?

Character…can you overcome the peer pressure to "fit in?" Do you drink? Do you Party?

Appearance…so you want to be a baseball player. Do you look like one? How do you carry yourself?

Demeanor…can you look people in the eye? Can you be respectful to others? Are you a good teammate?

As parents of professional and college athletes, we have seen so many gifted athletes defeat themselves by making poor choices and not ever allowing themselves to reach their own full potential. Control is about putting yourself in position to win, on and off the field.

When a Major League team came calling in our home town in 2004 they were preparing to make Justin their first choice in the draft and pay him millions of dollars. They never spoke to anyone about his baseball prowess--they already knew all about that. Instead, they called on our neighbors, our friends, coaches, teachers and folks in our small town of Goochland, Virginia. They asked questions like "Is he a good student? What kind of person is Justin? Does he party? Does he drink? Does he stay out late?"

After all, no one wants to make a job offer, grant a scholarship, or risk the reputation of their school, team, or business on someone without CONTROL.

There was an incident in Game Five of the 2011 American League Championship Series when the Tigers played the Texas Rangers at Comerica Park in Detroit. And unless you saw the game on TV, you've probably heard nothing of it. The question is, why?

It was an incident that had all the ingredients for sports figureheads and pundits to debate, gnashing and gnarling on and on about this and that, and yet it died quickly on the vine, the life sucked out of it by one of the principal players in the drama, Justin Verlander.

It was the top of the 8th inning, with one out, and a count of 0 balls, and 2 strikes. Verlander was on the mound, and at bat was Nelson Cruz, arguably the hottest hitter for the Rangers at the time. Verlander fired a 100 MPH fastball into the strike zone and Cruz connected to send the ball over the left-field fence for a two-run homer.

Fans got a double treat. For one thing, Verlander was over a hundred and thirty pitches into the game and he was still firing heat. For another, Cruz was on fire himself, and catching up to, and clearing the fence with, a 100 MPH fastball is a feat few players can boast. This was a point not lost on Cruz.

Major network cameras televising the game kept their focus on Cruz and Verlander well after the inning was over, and both players were in their dugouts. Closing in on Cruz, the camera caught the Rangers right fielder holding up his right index finger (one) and then forming an "0" twice with his left index finger and thumb (zero, zero). On camera, it looked as though Cruz was signaling over to Verlander in the opposing dugout that he had knocked Verlander's best pitch out of the park.

The announcers for the game quickly picked up on all of this and made the case that Cruz was mocking Verlander, or at least having fun at Verlander's expense.

After the game, while interviewing Verlander, this incident came up, and Verlander was given the chance to get back at Cruz.

But guess what; he didn't. He snuffed it, then and there. He laughed it off and said, "It's all good."

In an article entitled "Cardinals Realize Cruz Can Pull a Fast One" by Tim Brown of Yahoo! Sports on October 18, 2011, Verlander explained the situation like this:

"The pitch before, I blew one by him," Verlander said. "And then challenged him again. Made a mistake. ... Go look at all the home runs he's hit this series. I say all of them, because he's hit a few of them, and that's about the spot that he's hit them.

"And really, I out-thunk myself. I thought I made him look foolish on a couple of curveballs earlier in the game. Here I am – 0-and-2 – he might be sitting on another one. So, I'm playing that guessing game with him. ... Tried to sneak one by him and he was ready for it. That's in the air, it's, 'Please go foul. Please go foul. I'm such an idiot, please go foul.' It didn't."

The question is, why wasn't there more commotion about all this? Isn't this professional sports, where saving face and preserving sky-high egos is the name of the game? Why didn't Justin Verlander rip into Cruz and let the world know what he thought of Cruz's little stunt?

For the answer, we turn to Pat Ross, of Richmond, Virginia.

"Justin always focused on the task at hand."

"Huh?" you may ask, and "who is Pat Ross?"

Pat Ross is the father of Kevin Ross. Kevin Ross probably holds the distinction of having played more years of baseball with Justin Verlander than any other ball player. Starting with T-ball at age 8, and on through AAU and American Legion ball in the high school years, Kevin, a tall lefty first baseman, was always in the picture. And wherever Kevin was, his father, Pat, was never far behind.

If anyone witnessed the maturing of Justin Verlander as a ballplayer and a man as much as Justin's parents, it was Pat Ross. He was there when Justin hit his first T-ball. He was there when Justin hit the ball 240 feet over the fence as a 12-year old. He was there when Justin threw a pitch so hard that it broke his son Kevin's arm. And he was there at the game in Maryland, when as a 17-year-old, Justin threw a shut-out 1-0 game against the Orioleanders, a very tough team made up of Delaware and Maryland All-Stars.

But most importantly, Pat Ross was there to see how Justin was raised, and in Pat's words, Richard and Kathy just "did it right." As Pat says, "When you look at kids, you can't help but look at the parents. If the discipline isn't there, it shows."

"Don't take this the wrong way," says Pat, holding his hand out in front of him to make his point, "no one would ever mistake Richard Verlander as a baseball player." Pat's expression doesn't change. "In other words, it's not like Richard was ever a Major League ballplayer himself. He didn't "know the ropes." But what he did know was how to raise his kids, and he made the right moves. His kids are living proof of his and Kathy's hard work."

"Let me give you an example," says Pat. "One day one of the parents came over to Richard and said, 'Do you think Justin should play some other position other than pitcher?' It was a loaded question, and Richard realized it at the time. It was the kind of question that could very easily make a parent mad. Make you lose your cool, if you know what I mean. This parent thought that their kid was better than Justin, and they wanted Justin out of the way. I was always amazed at the way some parents reacted to Justin. They didn't see him as an asset to the team; they saw him as getting in the way of their own kid being in the limelight. You know, it wasn't the kids that felt that way, it was the parents!

Anyway, I saw how Richard handled what that parent had said to him. He didn't get mad. He didn't try to get even. What he did was use those words to strengthen his resolve to keep his focus on his own son and on his own actions as a parent. He never compared Justin to any of the other players, and he never allowed Justin to set goals higher than what he could reach at that moment in his development."

"Like the time a number of us parents were leaning against the fence watching a practice and one of the parents barked out, 'Don't you think if there were any Major League ballplayers out here, we'd know it by now?' The kids were 14 years old! Some were still in braces for crying out loud!"

"Richard never put pressure like that on Justin. It was always one obtainable goal at a time. Instead of the Major Leagues, Richard had Justin aiming to win his next game, or aiming to win the All-Star team, or something else that was attainable for his age and where he was in his development. It was always one step at a time, focusing on a particular goal. All else was fluff and a waste of time.

And that, dear reader, is the story behind how Justin Verlander found it easy to dismiss the dissing of Nelson Cruz. It's simply a matter of choosing where to place your focus.

Justin winds up to deliver in AAU
National Championship Game.
Sarasota, Florida, 1998.

Naysayers and Overcoming Negatives

You can't do that. You'll never make it. Chances are one in a million. You're too little. Too slow. Too skinny. Too fat. Too short. Too tall. You look funny. You aren't cool. You can't hit. Can't field. Can't throw. You're too wild. Don't you think you would know by now if you were that good?

RICHARD VERLANDER

Negative people will wear you out! Seeds won't grow in bad soil and sometimes you just need to move on.

As new parents, we learned some valuable lessons watching our Justin, our first child, grow up. Looking back, we didn't fully understand just how vital a role key people such as teachers, coaches, and other adult mentors play in raising confident kids. Like most parents, we ran across plenty of the glass half empty crowd; the gloom and doomers; the average and the ordinary, who seemed to think that it somehow raised their stature to bring others down. But we were also very blessed to have some extremely gifted educators and coaches as part of our life.

A key educator in Justin's early childhood was his second grade teacher, Marion Kramer. To this day I'm not sure she knows what an important role she played by seeing positive potential and instilling confidence in a young boy who had already been labeled by earlier teachers and others as being hyper, too fidgety, and disruptive, talking too much in class. We were advised to put him on medication that would help him calm down and "fit in" with the others. Justin didn't like school, and we were worried.

Coach Bob Smith and the Virginia AAU State Champion, Richmond Virginians, 1998.

I can't express how relieved Kathy and I were when we went in for Justin's second grade parent/teacher conference. Mrs. Kramer said, "Justin is a real handful, but I love him. He is very energetic and social. He is a good student when challenged with things that interest him and keep him focused and on task. I really think that one day all that energy will turn into something special."

Justin started to like school and his grades improved along with his feelings about his teacher. Mrs. Kramer taught a lot more than ABC's. She taught Justin that being unique is not a negative. It is something to be embraced and channeled in a positive atmosphere. It was a life defining time for our little son—and us!

Another defining moment came in the summer of 1998, when we were in Sarasota, Florida, for the 15U AAU Baseball Nationals. It was late in the game and we had a one run lead with one inning to go.

Now, bear in mind that this team was made up of extremely good ball players from all around the Richmond area. The talent was so strong that at this level and time in Justin's development, Justin was not the best player on the team. In fact, he really wasn't even the best pitcher. He could throw hard, but to say he had mastered control of his pitches would be an overstatement.

Yet at this critical stage of the game, the last inning and clinging to a one run lead, Coach Bob Smith called on Justin to pitch.

The coach's call sent shock waves through the stands. Kathy and I could sense the other parents rolling their eyes, shaking their heads and muttering, "What is the coach thinking? Justin is too wild! He needs at least a couple of innings to warm up! He will blow it. He walks too many batters! We heard from front and from behind. We were surrounded by naysayers from our own team, and they didn't seem to care that we heard.

But Justin did not lose that day. He shut down the opposing team and didn't walk a batter. We won the game!

Over the next several years Coach Smith, a former college coach and professional scout, was a vital component in Justin's development. We remain close.

So just what was Bob Smith thinking that hot afternoon in Florida?

"I knew Justin could do it," he later said. "I intentionally put him into a situation where I knew he would have to focus and throw strikes."

Bob Smith is another excellent example of how an important person in Justin's life showed confidence where others voiced negatives based on their perception of what Justin couldn't do.

Teachers, coaches, and other adult mentors are very much our partners in raising confident successful kids. Positive reinforcement is the fertile ground from which our kids can grow to their own full potential. Conversely, a negative, critical, pessimistic environment is a barren landscape from which even the hardiest seedlings struggle to grow and thrive. In hindsight, we were very lucky to have been blessed by some very special individuals in our lives that reinforced our own personal views about overcoming adversity, being positive, and celebrating special qualities that every son and daughter, in his or her own unique way, surely possesses.

If you stop to think about it, baseball is all about overcoming negatives. It's a sport in which a player who gets a hit three out of every ten at bats is considered among the best. To the naysayers, anyone who is unsuccessful at anything seven times out of ten would surely be labeled as a loser. As parents of two great kids, we realize that raising happy, eager, high achieving young people means that in life, like baseball, being positive is often about turning negatives inside out.

"I really think that one day all that energy will turn into something special."

Marion Kramer, Justin's second grade teacher at Gayton Elementary
School in Henrico County, Virginia

It takes a Village to Raise a Ballplayer!

"Individual commitment to a group effort, that is what makes a team work, a company work, a society work, a civilization work."

Vince Lombardi

I t's a fact; volunteers are the backbone that make it all work. These moms and dads put in countless hours shuffling their own often hectic schedules to prepare snacks, rake fields, fix "boo-boos," serve as taxi drivers and man the concession stands. They sell cookies and raffle tickets to each other for fundraisers. Oh, and they also coach!

Just like T-Ballers, new volunteers often struggle as "rookies," but progress into veterans around the ballpark after just a few years. The experienced volunteers teach the parents of the latest six and seven-year-olds just what they have gotten into by offering to "help out." After being taught by those who came before them, the established pros teach the newbies how to become experts at many tasks they never knew they could perform! Little League parents learn to become accomplished cooks, coaches, groundskeepers, doctors and painters. They become elected officials and scorekeepers (a very important job!). The hardiest souls even learn to be umpires!

What a great organization to witness and be a part of! If I can teach that mom over there who is a teacher at the elementary school how to teach the proper fielding techniques, maybe she can give me a clue how to impose some semblance of order in a ten year old dugout. And that dad who keeps score and works as an accountant sure turned into a good pitching coach, didn't he? The electrician who repaired the lights over on the ten-year-olds' field never played a sport in his life, but now he is our first base coach and is really good at working with the hitters.

And there's little Joey who lost his dad last year.... His mom has to work two jobs but still manages to be at every game. You should have seen his smile when coach gave him the game ball last week!

All of this activity sends a strong message to our youngsters about what it means to be part of a team, and that everyone has something to offer.

Having Fun and Hitting the Road
The AAU Years

Our days of traveling for baseball began when Justin turned thirteen. At the time, he was playing for the Richmond Virginians, a newly developed Amateur Athletic Union ("AAU") team that got its name from a New York Yankees Minor League franchise team that played in Richmond from 1954 to 1964 at Parker Field. Our AAU squad was comprised of extremely talented Little Leaguers from the Richmond area and was coached by a bunch of us dads that had little idea of how strong the competition would be at this level.

It wasn't too long before we found out just how strong. I, for one, can attest to the caliber of players we have in the State of Virginia, even at the age of thirteen. These other players were not only naturally talented, but their skills had been honed sharply by lots of practice and good coaching. If we hoped to reach our goal of advancing to the AAU National Tournament, we were going to have to qualify by competing against these other well-established and well-polished clubs.

To give you an idea of the caliber of players that we were up against, check out this list of future Major Leaguers: David Wright, Ryan Zimmerman, BJ Upton and Justin Upton, to name a few!

Fortunately for us, the top three teams in the state qualified for the AAU National Tournament. By defeating the Virginia Beach Blasters in an epic thirteen inning battle, we secured third place and earned our way into the National Tournament, held in Chickasha, Oklahoma (the watermelon capital of the world). Once there, our boys finished fourth in the nation. Not bad for our first year in the league!

The Virginians would continue to play together as a team, advancing to the National Tournament again as fourteen and fifteen year olds. Many of the players went on to play college baseball, and some played, or are still playing, as professionals.

Just as importantly, many have gone on to very successful careers in the corporate world, or as doctors, lawyers, coaches and teachers. Many of them point to their days as part of the "V's" as instrumental in developing tools that would help later on as they continued their quest for excellence in other parts of their lives.

Yard Sale

As the saying goes, there are three important things to remember when considering real estate--location, location, location.

The same rule applies when considering sites for a yard sale.

Justin was thirteen years old and was pitching for a Richmond area AAU team called the Richmond Virginians. I was helping manage the team, and I modestly say that we were pretty darn good. Motivated players filled each position and all summer long the practices had been hard, fun, and productive. The time and effort that these kids put into pitching, hitting and fielding paid off, and the team earned the opportunity to play for the national championship in Chickasha, Oklahoma.

The only problem was, we had to pay our own way to get there.

For some of the kids, money was no problem. Heck, I expect their fathers could have written a check for the whole team. Team spirit was at such a high that I expect they would have, too, if I had asked, but what kind of lesson would have come from that? There had to be a better way.

It was Kathy and some of the other mothers who came up with the solution.

"Let's have a yard sale!" Their enthusiasm was contagious. Everyone agreed that it was a great idea--but where?

One of the fathers piped up. "We'll have it at my place!"

I looked at him kind of funny, and he gave me a puzzled look back.

"Isn't your house at the end of a cul-de-sac?" I asked.

"Not at my house," he laughed. "At my business! It's out on Route 1 and the traffic going up and down that road is tremendous. We'll have more people stopping by than we can handle!"

Location, location, location. I felt better.

***

Advertisements had appeared in the paper, flyers had been stapled to telephone poles all over town, and huge yellow, green and red posters plastered Route 1 to the north and south.

HUGE YARD SALE!

SATURDAY

8:00 - 1:00

"I've never seen so much stuff in all my life," said Kathy. Her expression was a mix of awe and delight. There's nothing like having a successful idea and having it take off and become a reality. And boy did this idea take off! It was a home run.

It was seven a.m. and the sun was already shining bright on what promised to be another hot summer day. Most everybody was dressed in shorts and T-shirts and had already worked up a sweat unpacking their wares and laying them out on blankets, card tables, and boards straddling sawhorses.

Kathy and a couple of other mothers counted out cash from the lockbox to prepare for the change we'd need, and I mentally practiced my haggling and negotiation techniques, honed from years of negotiating labor contracts for C&P Telephone employees. I was in my element.

I decided to survey the territory and take a few minutes to do a sweep of the perimeter.

Kathy was right. There was an incredible amount of stuff here. And what a variety! Over here was the doctor's section. Gee whiz! I was tempted to buy these things myself. There were Persian rugs, a beautiful stained glass lamp, and all kinds of things that would perk up our living room. Then the lawyer next to him had handsome leather-bound books and fireplace andirons and utensils that looked brand new. And it went on from there: the teachers with their kitchen appliances; the businessmen with their lawn equipment; and those who I knew were struggling to get by, they had glass and plate sets, sport memorabilia, old record players, albums, gym equipment… It was all so amazing!

Everyone was here, and everyone contributed. And everyone was having fun!

I had circled around and was back to where Kathy was handling the cash from one of the first customers. There was something special going on here. This was more than a yard sale. This was a community pitching together, contributing what they can to reach a common goal, to attain a higher good. Was I the only one that got what was going on here?

"You gonna stand there all day?"

"Huh?"

It was Kathy. "Go over and help those customers!"

As I turned to move in the direction of Kathy's pointing finger, I caught her smiling.

She got it.

Today the traveller on the Nile enters a wonderland at whose gates rise the colossal pyramids of which he has had visions perhaps from earliest childhood.

James H. Breasted, American archaeologist and historian.

The Pyramid Of Success

When people hear Justin say that his goal is the Hall of Fame and that every time he pitches he expects to throw a no-hitter, it always gives one pause to reflect. Is this guy that arrogant? What an ego! Was he raised that way or did he let success go to his head? What must his parents think???

Having spent much of my life around very successful individuals in many different arenas I have come to the conclusion that many of us tend to rush to judgment about those who are at the top of their craft. Perceived "cockiness" is often confidence in disguise, or merely the expression of the self-expectations of high achievers.

Internally, this would better be characterized as "drive" and reflects the traits that push or motivate these individuals to reach for ever higher goals.

While gaining experience in my own profession I learned that striving to be the best for me is more often an inward look at fulfillment that is based on pushing to overcome limiting self-perceptions. What I learned is that for me real success is measured incrementally and that the affirmations of goals are results.

In this fashion achievement becomes a pyramid—one building block of accomplishment on top of another, each level creating a higher expectation based upon the confidence gained by fulfilling the goal of completing today's level to the very best of your ability. Viewed in that context, would it be unreasonable or arrogant for an All-American college football player to state that his goal, or next level of the pyramid, is to win the Heisman Trophy? For a hard working high school student who was named to the National Honor Society to set a goal to be the first in her family to graduate college? For a new governor to be the first female president of the United States?

As parents, we have endeavored to instill in our boys the notion that striving to be the best you can be at the level you are at today, and successfully completing the current level of the pyramid, will lead to self-confidence, and more importantly, an expanded view of what is possible in the future. Even the Hall of Fame.

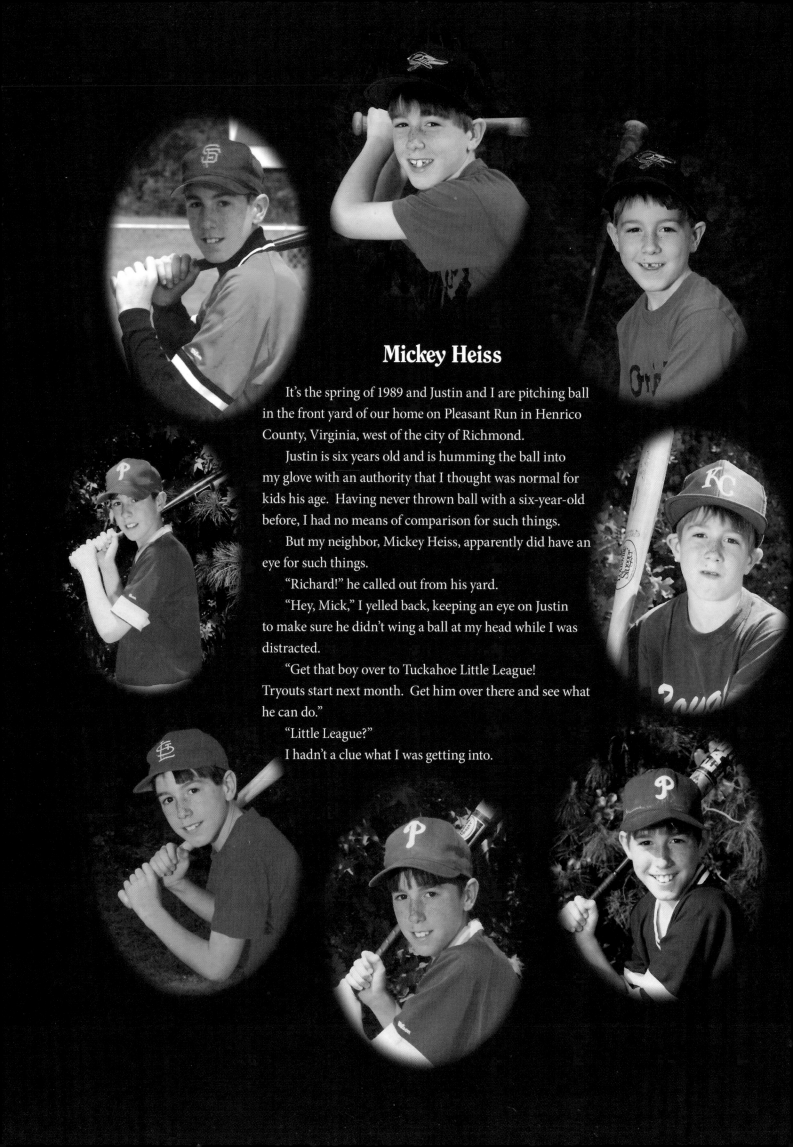

Mickey Heiss

It's the spring of 1989 and Justin and I are pitching ball in the front yard of our home on Pleasant Run in Henrico County, Virginia, west of the city of Richmond.

Justin is six years old and is humming the ball into my glove with an authority that I thought was normal for kids his age. Having never thrown ball with a six-year-old before, I had no means of comparison for such things.

But my neighbor, Mickey Heiss, apparently did have an eye for such things.

"Richard!" he called out from his yard.

"Hey, Mick," I yelled back, keeping an eye on Justin to make sure he didn't wing a ball at my head while I was distracted.

"Get that boy over to Tuckahoe Little League! Tryouts start next month. Get him over there and see what he can do."

"Little League?"

I hadn't a clue what I was getting into.

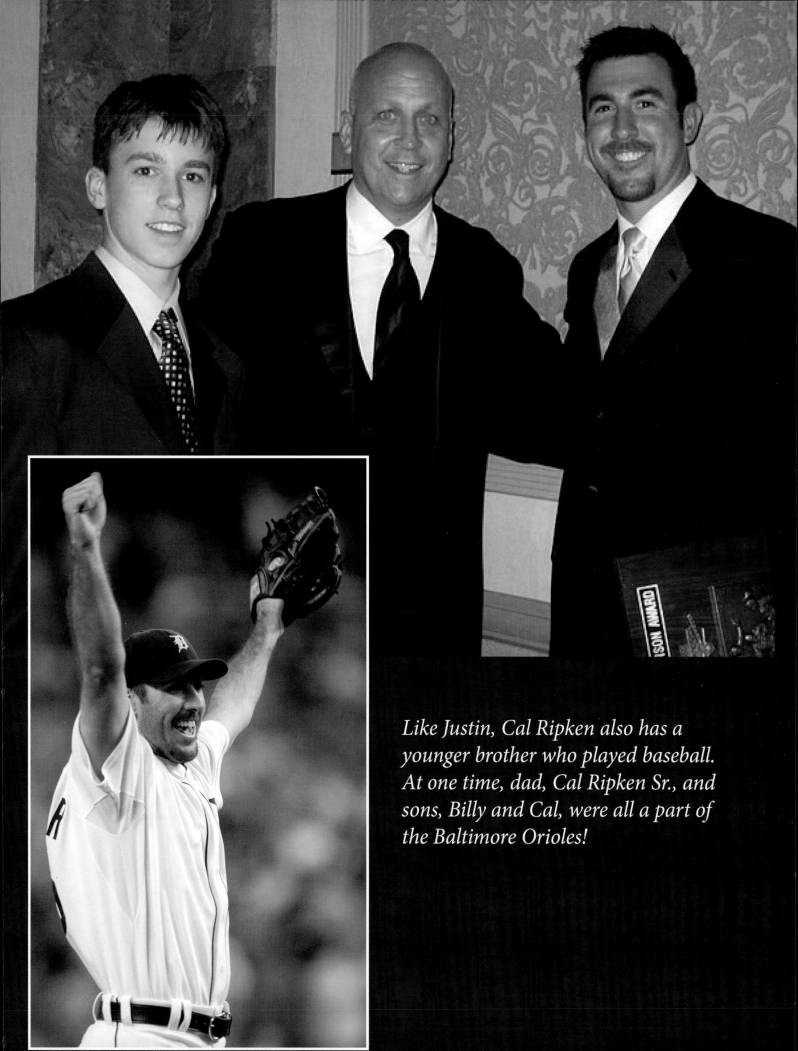

Like Justin, Cal Ripken also has a younger brother who played baseball. At one time, dad, Cal Ripken Sr., and sons, Billy and Cal, were all a part of the Baltimore Orioles!

"My God, that guy's throwing 10[0] miles an hour in the sixth inning[,] you're not going to mount much[?] against him. It's really tough for[?] the best hitters in baseball to pu[t] that in play consistently."

Atlanta Braves third basem[an] Chipper Jones: "Verlander, Tig[ers] silence Braves' bats again in wi[n]" Sports.espn.go.co[m] June 23, 20[11]

Justin Verlander

"He's the most dominating pitcher in the game right now...."

—Hall of Fame pitcher Nolan Ryan as quoted by Gerry Fraley, The Dallas Morning News, Inc., Oct. 7, 2011

Justin gets an ice-water shower following 2011 Mother's Day No-hitter versus Milwaukee Brewers. Fox Detroit Newspaper *Observer*.

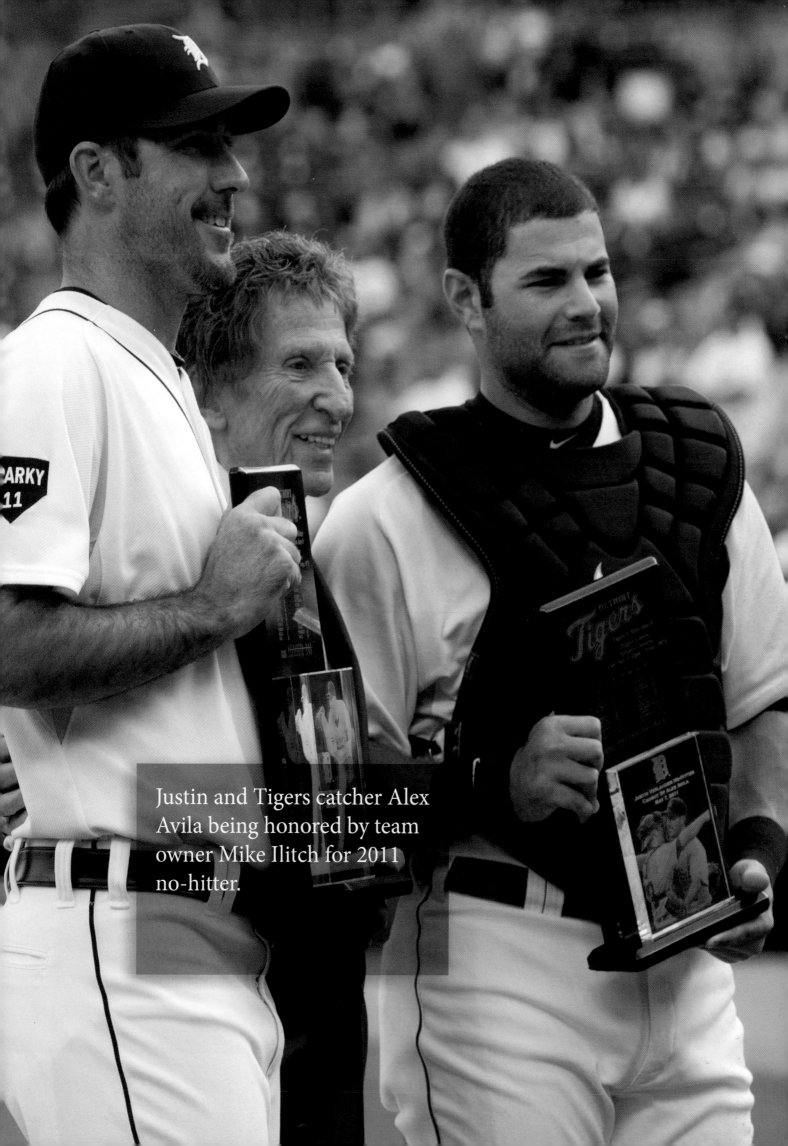

Justin and Tigers catcher Alex Avila being honored by team owner Mike Ilitch for 2011 no-hitter.

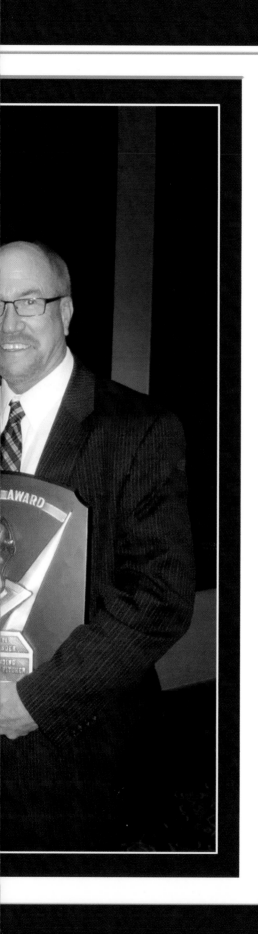

"Emily Yuen, Justin Verlander, Kathy Verlander and Richard Verlander following the presentation of the Cy Young and AL MVP Awards at the 2012 Baseball Writers Awards Banquet in New York City

Tuckahoe Little League
debut 1989
T-Ball Orioles

1993 all star
Tuckahoe Little League
Age 10

Goochland HS
All-Region, All-District
1998-2001

Detroit Tigers
2004
1st Pick MLB

1

Ju

Milw

American Legion Post 201
Graduate of the Year

Lakeland Tigers
Erie Seawolves
2005 FSL All-Star

1st Tir

1994 All Star
Tuckahoe Little League
Majors

Old Dominion University
Freshman All-American
2002

18

1995 All Star
Tuckahoe Little League
Majors

Old Dominion University
All Conference
2003-2004

Major League Debut
July 4th, 2005
@ Cleveland Indians

2n

Leads ML

1996 AAU
4th in Nation

and

Old Dominion University
Male Athlete of the Year
2004

Tigers
25 man roster
2006

3r

1

1997 AAU
VA State Champs

Detroit Tigers 2006
World Series starter
Tigers/MLB R.O.Y.

1998 AAU
Va. State Champs

vers

tar Team

RA

ar

ike-Outs

ar

A

2nd Career No Hitter
June 7, 2011
Toronto Blue Jays

2011
Cy Young Award
AL Triple Crown

2011
Sporting News
Player of the Year

2011
AL MVP Award

Players Choice Award
MLB 2K 12 Cover

How Much is too Much?

If your parents are too involved in your sport, they can make your life miserable,
kill your enjoyment and absolutely ruin your athletic performance.

Dr. Alan Goldberg, "Do you have Winning Parents?"

Parents of Little Leaguers often ask how to know when to "push," and when to "back off," when it comes to their young athlete. The very fact that they ask the question usually indicates that they understand there is a point where they may put too much pressure on their sons and daughters to perform and take away the fun.

Baseball is a great game and when played and taught properly can also be a great vehicle for parents to teach valuable life lessons to their children. The value of seeing the rewards of hard work is not the least of these. But the thing to remember is this is also a game. If the kids don't enjoy it, as soon as they are old enough, they will simply tell mom and dad, "I don't want to play anymore."

Now, sometimes you do need to push. If little Becky makes a commitment to be on the team, then she should not be allowed to skip practice when she doesn't feel like going, unless there is a good reason. If she pouts or throws a temper tantrum after striking out, she should be told that such behavior is not acceptable. And if young Johnny is bragging to anyone who will listen about how good he is at shortstop, counsel him on being humble. If on the way home from a big game they complain about the outfielder who dropped that pop-fly, teach them not to blame others.

We always have felt that making practice fun is a great way to keep Little Leaguers focused, and that "playing games" or competing with a friend during practice is a great way to accomplish that. On the other hand, telling junior that if he doesn't field 25 ground balls in a row he will have to run laps is a great way to get kids to hate baseball!

As our youngsters grow and mature, advancing in their academic, athletic, and professional careers, the stakes and the pressure to perform get higher. So let them be young while they can. If we have done our jobs as parents, they will never lose sight of the importance of balancing quality of life while climbing the corporate ladder, building their fortune, or winning the game of life.

Snack Time

It was a hot Saturday afternoon in mid-July and the two Little League teams had been playing hard through five and a half innings––two hours of running down fly, balls, sliding into base, and swinging at pitches.

It was the bottom of the sixth inning now, generally the end of regulation unless the game was tied, in which event the game would go into extra innings.

Justin was on the mound and had the lead, 5-4. There were two outs, with men on the corners at first and third. If Justin could get his last batter out, he'd have the win, and his team would be a game over .500 for the season. Not bad, given that they had lost so many games in the first part of the season, and were now making a strong comeback. If they kept it up, they could maybe even make the play-offs.

"STRIKE ONE!" cried the umpire, flailing his right arm out by his side like he was signaling a first down in football. A bit on the dramatic side, I thought, but he had called a fair game, so to each his own.

The catcher threw the ball back to Justin and I studied the man on first. He was a little guy, but a fast one. He had hit a ball to right field earlier in the game and most any other player would have gotten only to second. But this guy didn't hesitate. He flew around second and slid into third way ahead of the relay throw.

I wondered if Justin remembered how fast this little sucker was. Second was empty. There was a good chance that the opposing coach would flash the steal sign.

"Ball one," said the umpire, with little fanfare.

Heck, Justin was firing away. I wonder if he's even thinking about the guy on first. I mean, if the guy steals second, then the tying run is in scoring position. A base hit and the other team would win the game. Is Justin considering all of this?

"Ball two."

Oh no. Two balls and one strike. We don't need to walk this guy. A walk and the bases are loaded. We don't want to load the bases.

Justin gloves the throw from the catcher and walks back toward the top of the mound.

The adrenalin is pulsing through me like molten lava. The pressure is incredible. Two balls, one strike, man on third, fast guy on first...

Wait a minute! What if the guy on first does try to steal second? What is the play? Justin and I were watching a game the other night and when the man on first took off to steal second, the man on third stole home! It was a cake walk because the catcher had thrown the ball down to second to try to pick off the guy stealing, and the guy on third just practically walked home. It was wide open. Did Justin remember that? Does the catcher know what to do? Should I say something? Should I remind the coach to be on the lookout? What if they try a squeeze play at the plate? What if...

"I got it!"

I looked up and the third baseman was gathering underneath a pop fly. He caught the ball easily and the team came running off the field, over toward where Kathy and several other mothers had spread out some orange slices, granola bars and juice boxes.

I caught up with Justin as he was rounding the fence.

"Good game there, son!" I put my arm around his shoulders.

"Thanks, Dad."

"Pretty tight situation there at the end, eh?"

Justin looked up at me quizzically. "Huh?"

"I mean the men on the corners, the fast guy on first, the possibility of a steal, the chance of a squeeze play at the plate..."

"If you say so, Dad." Justin looked over my shoulder toward Kathy and the other mothers.

"Aw, man...granola bars again?"

Justin is 3rd from left, top row.

A Team, B Team, Red Team, Blue Team

Are you majoring in minors?

It usually starts in Little League. First it was majors vs. minors and the ever prestigious, my son is "playing up!" After that there was travel ball, All-Stars and showcase teams. Oh, and let's not forget the Gold Team, never to be confused with the Blue Team, or was it the 'A' Team that was the epitome?

Surely when your child gets to high school being on the Varsity as a freshman is an indicator of future stardom, right? And speaking of high school or college aspirations, shouldn't your son go to the "big name" schools? After all, college recruiters and professional scouts don't look for prospects at inferior programs do they?

In hindsight we realize that the perceived ultimate or elite status associated with playing for certain teams, schools, or programs is not necessarily an indicator of future success, and can even be detrimental in some instances. Some of these environments are geared too much toward their own prestige than they are being the best atmosphere for a young athlete to grow in. Our experience has taught us that playing for good coaches, and learning how to play the game the right way, in a nurturing environment that promotes individual growth and teamwork is far more important than labels. After all, who will care ten years from now that your daughter played for the "Honeybees" as a fifteen year old?

When recalling our family's journey, being the parents of little boys with big dreams, we remember a lot more about the people that played key roles in our sons' development than we do the names of the places, or teams that they played on. Keep your eye on the long range dreams and goals and use them as the basis for making the right choices now.

WHO YOUR CHILDREN PLAY FOR AND THE ATMOSPHERE THAT SURROUNDS THEM IS MUCH MORE IMPORTANT THAN WHERE THEY PLAY.

Justin and his high school team, The Goochland Bulldogs, coached by Bryan Gordon, Goochland County, Va.

Flying Flucos

Pull out a map of Virginia. Now, show me where the town of Fluvanna is. Well, unless you're from there, you're not going to know that this is a trick question. Fluvanna isn't a town. It is a county in Virginia.

One interesting tidbit about Fluvanna County is that it is the home of the town of Columbia, which way back when was a bustling community on the confluence of the James and Rivanna rivers. Centered in the middle of the Commonwealth of Virginia, local lore holds that it at one time received heavy consideration to be the state capital, missing its chance by only one vote. Columbia's main draw was the canal system, a major mode of transportation for coal and crops. Because of the fork in the water flow, caused by the two rivers coming together, it was necessary to cross over the Rivanna in order to keep on trucking, if you will, up the canal, which bordered the north side of the James. Borrowing from the Romans, the Fluvannans built a huge aqueduct that took the water out of the James, lifted it over the Rivanna, and brought it back down to the James so that the tradesmen wouldn't have to take their boat, and the merchandise on it, out of the water. It was the most amazing thing in Fluvanna County, but it was destroyed years ago through an act of legislation (and not by Union soldiers, though they tried).

Such were my thoughts as I took up my accustomed vantage point for Justin's ballgames—leaning against the light pole in right field, just beyond the first base coach's box. Only, this light pole wasn't as comfortable and familiar to me because we weren't at home for this game. It was an away game, the first of Justin's senior year, and Justin was slated to pitch for Goochland. And yes, it was in Fluvanna County. Fluvanna High School. FHS. Home of the Flying Flucos. I hear you giggling. I'm not making this up.

Okay, so I've had some fun, but the point is, Fluvanna County is not New York, Los Angeles, or Chicago, or any other place that you'd think would draw a crowd to see a budding high school pitcher. And yet, here they were, bunched up in the stands and lined up along the fence behind home plate: khaki pants, logo-crested baseball caps, and radar guns, all pointing at Justin on the mound like he was facing a firing squad. There must have been two dozen of them. Talent scouts from colleges across the nation and more than a few from professional teams.

They'd aim their guns, take some notes, aim their guns again, and take some more notes. It's a wonder Justin could concentrate on the game. I know I sure couldn't, not with the circus that was going on behind home plate.

One thing I know for sure, though. These scouts, as busy and important as they are, know how to find Fluvanna High School. And they can find your son or daughter too; I can assure you of that.

Get noticed by being a good teammate.

So How Does My Kid Get Noticed?

Make yourself stand out by realizing that if better is possible, then good is not enough

As far as getting noticed goes, baseball is no different than any other field of pursuit. Whether your young athlete is a current player, a prospect, or both, the answer to getting noticed is simple. They have to stand out from the crowd.

Whatever the endeavor, be it getting into a choice school, playing a sport on a college scholarship, or landing that dream job, there are some things over which you simply have no control. For example, not everyone throws a baseball 95 MPH. Fortunately, there are many other elements involved in getting your youngster some positive attention.

We have had the good fortune over the years to come to know many professional scouts and college coaches and have attended many tryouts and camps where there were a hundred or more very talented athletes vying for attention. To even the untrained eye there are usually two or three that stand out due to sheer physical gifts. But guess what? Two or three do not go far in making out a roster for the several college coaches in attendance. The art of scouting and recruiting is spotting the players in the crowd that make for a good TEAM.

Someone from the sea of talented and skilled players that will demonstrate to the scouts that they will contribute, and reflect well on the coaches and the program. Someone that is likely to do what is necessary to be successful, when the spotlight is not turned on them.

"Okay!" your eager, chomping at the bit, future all-star exclaims. "But what are they looking for? How do I separate myself from the crowd? How can I be special?"

By arriving early and staying late

By being a good teammate

By being sincere

By hustling

By cleaning out the dugout when no one is watching

By chasing foul balls

By making eye contact

By listening

By having your hat on straight and your pants pulled up

By saying "thank you"

By not wearing pajamas to practice (saw it I swear!)

By complimenting others

By being humble

By being a leader

By not following the crowd

By thinking for yourself

By doing more than is required

By being gracious in defeat

By having a firm handshake

So, there simply are no secret tricks to getting noticed. The old cliché, "being in the right place at the right time" doesn't matter one iota if you don't stand out. And you stand out by being special!

Ben at ODU Camp

How you act matters, especially if you are trying to stand out in a positive way.

Richard Verlander

When Ben, our youngest son, was sixteen years old, and a sophomore at Goochland High School, he attended an instructional baseball camp at Old Dominion University in Norfolk, Virginia.

ODU may ring a bell. It is where Justin went to college.

Now, there are many instructional camps, in Virginia and elsewhere, that Ben could have attended. At first glance it may seem that Ben chose an easy path--going to camp at the same place that his older brother had such success. Surely the Verlander name would make this a cake walk.

Nothing could have been further from the truth. When he got to the camp, the coaches came up to Ben and said, "We know who you are, but there it stops. As far as Ben Verlander goes, you are in the same spot that all of the other players are in. You were invited here because of the player you have become and what you have accomplished in the classroom."

Ben preferred it this way. If anything, he knew that he had to perform that much better to be noticed for his own accomplishments, and not just those of his older brother.

And when the camp was over, Ben did get noticed. Sure, his baseball skills were fine, but they weren't what set him apart. When the coaches talked to us about Ben, what stuck out to them was the leadership he showed during the practices. It was his attitude and demeanor that caught their attention. That after practices Ben would shake hands of the other players and thank the coaches--those were the traits that stuck out.

As further evidence that how you act is as important as whether or not you can turn a double play, read this from a memorandum by Chris Finwood, Head Baseball Coach at ODU to his incoming baseball players:

Hard work, competing, doing the right things on and off the field, your attitude, and your performance will be key factors in each individual's evaluation…. Remember that who you are and what you do speak much more loudly than what you say.

So, make it a point to watch how you act and how you treat others. It makes a difference, and yes, people are watching.

Ben on signing day.

57

Practice what you Preach!

You need to show up early and stay late, hit the weights and run every day! You have to get tougher! Play through the pain! Work harder!" Great advice and a strong message, right dad? Well, there's only one problem... HE'S EIGHT YEARS OLD!!!

Richard Verlander

Baseball is a tough game to play, but is also a great vehicle for teaching youngsters important life skills. It is very important to understand the age appropriateness of lessons that are best taught through observation as young athletes mature, as opposed to lectures and speeches that are often too much to comprehend. When we look back now it is apparent that well meaning parents often put way too much emphasis on force-feeding adult attributes to young athletes who are likely more concerned about the post game snack than they are about their work ethic.

Traits such as work ethic, drive, leadership, and ambition are best acquired over time by observing these behaviors in their adult role models, rather than having them force-fed to youngsters at the expense of having fun. That's right, fun! When the game is no longer fun, it is usually because of overbearing adults, and by the time our kids are old enough to say, "I just don't like baseball anymore," it's over.

Let's say it again; adult qualities should be NURTURED and ENCOURAGED through example, not force-fed.

So...

Are YOU always on time? Do YOU finish what you start? Do YOU go the extra mile? Do YOU volunteer to help? Are YOU a quitter? Do YOU work hard? Do YOU take care of your body? Are YOU a team player? Are YOU humble? Are YOU a positive person? Can YOU handle failure? Are YOU passionate about your work? Do YOU follow your dreams? Can YOU handle adversity? Do YOU show your temper? Do YOU honor commitments? Are YOU respectful of others? and... DO YOU KNOW HOW TO HAVE FUN???

59

Tuckahoe Little League Off-Season

There are few places more peaceful than a ball diamond in the off-season. No bats cracking hits, no infielders cracking jokes, and no fans eating Cracker Jacks. It's just the freshly mowed grass and neatly raked dirt infield, all fenced in and protected from the outside world.

On many fall afternoons, long after the hustle and bustle of the summer baseball season had ended, my friend Pat Ross and I would take the boys over to the Tuckahoe Little League fields to get in some practice. We'd take a bucket of balls, a bat or two, gloves and water bottles and practice hitting, fielding, and pitching. We would come up with different games to make it fun and before we knew it, it would be time for dinner.

When I look back on those days, I remember that I've never sweat so much having fun. We were outside, getting exercise, playing made-up games and constantly getting better at a sport that we all loved. We were training and improving all the time but really didn't know it because it was all wrapped in so much fun.

And now, when Pat Ross and I talk about those sunny afternoons spent at the ballpark in the off-season, we always come back to the same question: how come there was nobody else out there?

Bob Wojnowski, columnist Detroit News

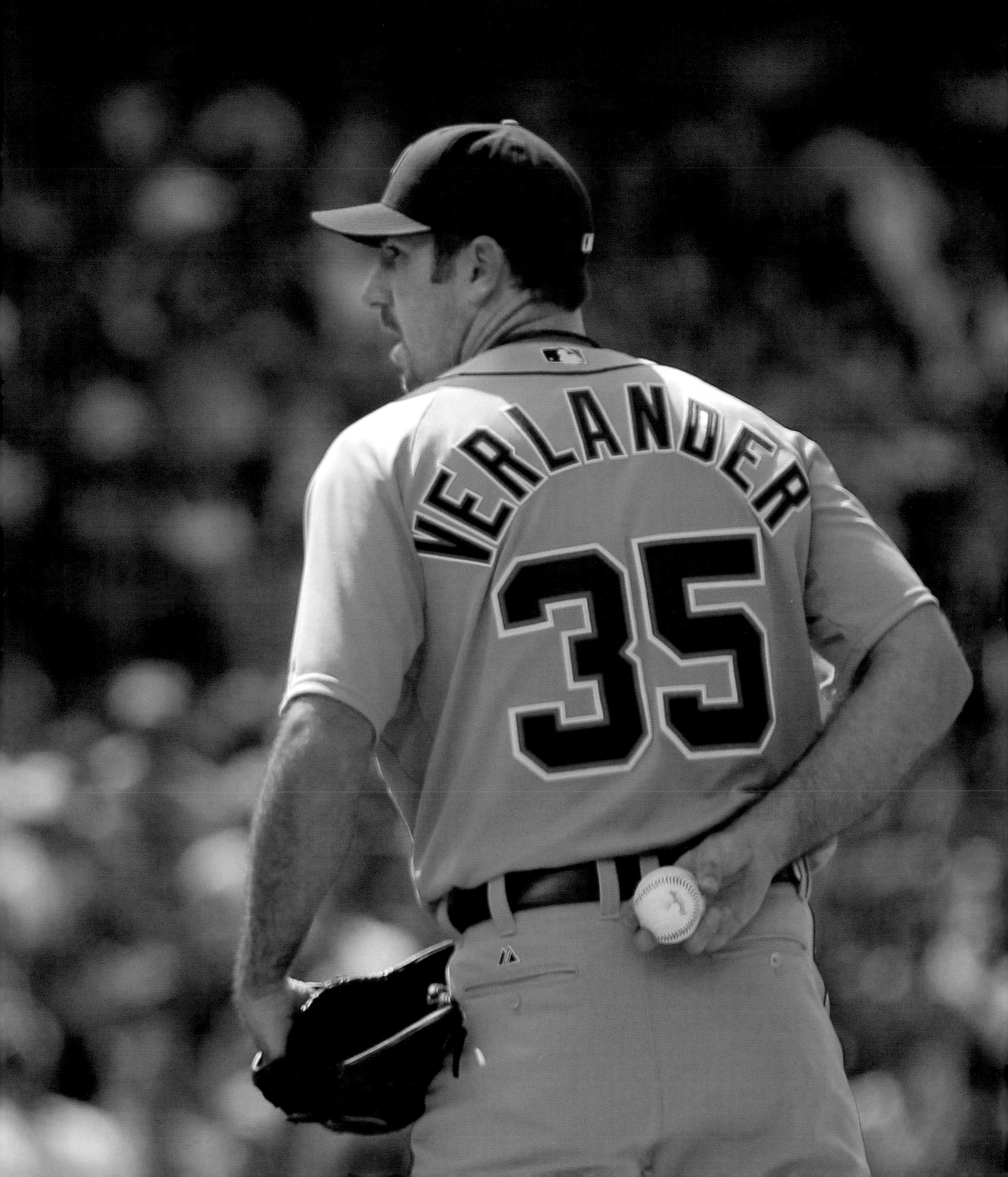

Sports Illustrated

SEPTEMBER HEAT

Flamethrowing (101 mph) Justin Verlander And the Amazing Tigers Say

BRING IT

BY TOM VERDUCCI

"Pinch Me" Moments

People often ask us: "What's it like to be the parents of an MLB All-Star? When did you first know? Are there any special moments or places that stand out when you first thought, WOW! Justin could be a Major Leaguer?"

To answer these questions, we must first explain that there have been many memorable experiences and events that have caused us to pause and catch our breath, shaking our heads in disbelief at some of the sheer physical gifts that our young son possesses.

For instance, there was the time when Justin was nine years old and we were at a local park skipping rocks across a pond. Young Justin left us slack-jawed when he hurled one from shore to shore over a distance that dad could not come close to approaching! Then there was the Little League playoff game when as a ten year old he faced down some of the toughest twelve year olds in the league with that glare that is now so famous. Or the first time he reached back and threw 86 MPH as a fifteen year old on a showcase team. The ball bounced off the helmet of a very imposing college-bound senior, went over the backstop, down a hill, and disappeared into a lake! Fortunately, the batter was okay. And later, there was the time he reached 98 MPH on a radar gun as I stared in disbelief over the shoulder of a Major League scout who didn't seem to believe what he was seeing either! Towards the end of the 2004 season these scouts showed up in such numbers you wouldn't believe! With their radar guns raised in unison as Justin wound up to deliver the ball home the scene more resembled a Shoot Out at OK Coral than a college baseball game! Moments in time; the stuff of fantasy: number one draft pick, TV, All-Stars, Rookie of the Year Award, parades, the World Series, American League Cy Young and MVP awards…it's more than a parent can get their head around!

So with all of this going on, are there any moments that are more special than the rest, that as parents we are more proud of than any of the others? Moments that are truly "pinch me moments"?

Well, yes…and those moments don't involve ESPN, radar readings, championships, or All-Star games.

The answer lies in the light that we see in the eyes of a kid who is last in line after a long day of signing autographs; in the feeling of joy we get from seeing fancy shoes from an endorsement contract being donated to a Lakeland, Florida orphanage; in the random, unsolicited compliments paid to us about our son by field workers or other Minor League personnel who remember Justin fondly from so many years ago. It's in the warmth that we experience when we are honored by the family of an injured Veteran who has had exclusive use of Justin's luxury suite at Comerica Park; and in the blessings we receive from people in Detroit who so generously and genuinely thank us for raising such a good person—one who brings hope to a city that has endured so much.

When it comes down to what really makes us the most proud (as is the case with most parents), it's about the young men and women we have raised, and the things they do with their gifts to make life better for others.

Now those are "PINCH ME MOMENTS!"

Justin was selected to pitch for Team USA in the Pan-Am Games in Santa Domingo, Dominican Republic in 2003.

Justin and teammates at auto factory in Detroit.

Justin gets a shaving cream pie following his no hitter versus the Milwaukee Brewers.

Clemente Award

Justin has won many awards and reached so many milestones in his Major League Baseball career, but there is one award that I have not mentioned. Ironically, it is an award that Justin did not win. Nonetheless, it is one of the distinctions bestowed upon Justin for which we are most proud because it recognizes not only Justin Verlander as an athlete, but Justin Verlander as a contributor to society.

I am referring to the Roberto Clemente Award. Much as the man for whom the honorarium is named, this Award is unique. It goes beyond balls and strikes, RBI's and home runs. It looks beyond the score sheet and takes into account the player himself, and what he's contributed to the team, and to the community. It takes into account what's truly important.

Few people know this, but Justin has his own box suite at Comerica Park, the Tigers' home stadium in downtown Detroit. On days that Justin pitched the suite often sat empty as friends and family would sit behind home plate. Justin took note of this and decided to do something about it.

He got together with the local Veterans Affairs and asked them to invite the families of injured soldiers from Iraq and Afghanistan to his suite on the days that he pitched. Before long, crowds of veterans and their families were filling Justin's suite and yelling and rooting like crazy! What was once an empty shell on Justin's pitching days is now a bustling cheering section for the home team! They even have a name: Verlander's Victory for Veterans.

Like the veterans who honor Justin by sitting in his suite, the Tiger organization recognizes what is truly important. And that is why having our son be the Detroit Tigers nominee for the 2011 Roberto Clemente Award is such an honor.

View From A Friend

by
Steve Watson

Outside of the locker room in the lower recesses of Comerica Park, standing under a sign that reads, "Family and Friends of Players," I can't help but feel that I'm part of something special. "Family and friends," and I'm standing here waiting for Justin Verlander. And I know he's coming. Holy Toledo! as they say when so close to the Ohio line, this is cool!

The first player that I recognize is Brandon Inge. He's not as tall as you'd think he'd be, but still, there's a presence, a glow, if you will, that here's someone special. The eye is naturally drawn to him, even though he's just chatting with one of the stadium security guards.

Next comes Miguel Cabrera, and he is as big as I thought he'd be. He comes out all smiles and starts high-fiving and yucking it up with the small crowd of family and friends that have been waiting across the hall for him.

They continue their chatter as they head up the hallway toward the players' car garage.

And then I see him. A tall, dark shadow at first—black hair, dark facial hair, dark eyes, black t-shirt, weathered-looking blue jeans and black shoes—approaching from the hallway behind Richard, Justin's father.

"There he is," I say, and Richard immediately cuts off the conversation and swings around to greet his son.

The dark figure that had loomed in the shadowy hallway only moments before is now standing before his father, all smiles and warmth. A warmth that is reserved for, and certainly displayed only before those that are close family. It's a treat to observe, and again, I'm reminded that I am part of something special.

Fittingly, Justin and his father embrace, and, if only for a moment, all the cares of the day are washed away, and the core values of love between father and son take the stage.

It dawns on me, is it this value, this importance of relationships, of concern and love for one another, that fans, young and old alike, rich and poor, see in Justin Verlander? Is this what draws the city of Detroit to Comerica Park?

Could it be that simple?

"Identity" Theft

I'm not sure when it happened, but at some point along the way we stopped being Richard and Kathy and became…*Justin Verlander's mom and dad.*

That's who we are now.

Don't get me wrong, this is a role that we proudly embrace, but it does take some getting used to! My old boss used to jokingly refer to me as "Justin's dad" in meetings or when introducing me to colleagues. Everywhere we go, be it to a doctor's appointment, a cookout, or to make an acquaintance we are quickly identified by the new title!

Hey! That's Justin Verlander's mom and dad!

Even our identity as parents can be challenged when success comes early for our offspring. While feeling very blessed in the knowledge that our son's future is secure at an early age, we also sometimes feel (to put it in football terms) that we "missed the handoff"—the gradual transfer of dependence that defines the typical parenting experience.

So you parents that are caught up in the glow of your children's success, remember not to lose sight of your own accomplishments, careers, and achievements. Be proud of the role you have played! Raising successful kids is a product of your life's body of work, but don't let it identify who *YOU* are.

And that goes for siblings as well. Our son Benjamin, who is very proud of his brother, has done a great job of carving his own space and is special for his own unique qualities.

At the end of the day we will always be Mom and Dad to our boys.

And isn't that the important thing?

Richard Verlander being interviewed by Dana Wakiji, Detroit News sport writer.

Courtesy of Getty Images

Positioned For Success

"It would kill some men to get that close
to their dream and not touch it. They'd consider it a tragedy.."

"Son, if I'd only gotten to be a doctor for five minutes...
...now that would have been a tragedy."

(Moonlight Graham – Field Of Dreams)

When young players are growing up playing baseball they all want to be the pitcher or the shortstop. Like being the quarterback on the football team, it is a well-established tradition that of all the positions, these are the most glamorous! After all, isn't that where the "best" players play?

Over time, of course, our job as parents is to encourage our youngsters to look beyond "labels" and discover what position, college, field of study, or calling they aspire to is best based on their own unique skills and personalities and what they are passionate about.

Being positioned for success can sometimes mean holding on to values that ground them when they suddenly find themselves in the spotlight of fame and fortune. Parents, family and old friends are a constant in a sudden whirlwind life. People who can keep budding superstars grounded by reminding them that they can still mow the lawn, take out the trash, and act a fool every now and then.

These are also the people who remind them that the significance of their deeds will be remembered far longer than the substance that comes with fame, and that true success comes from fulfillment.

"Leave the dugout cleaner than you found it and make the world a better place."

Vranian at the Plate

It takes heart to play baseball. No one knows this better than Cardiologist Michael Vranian, M.D. Hearts are his specialty. But to get to where he is today, he had to pass an important test.

The medical board exam: the one test and the one chance to determine the direction that Michael Vranian's life would take after so many years of medical school.

Vranian had always wanted to be a cardiologist. He knew it would take hard work, and as his friends said, he'd have to "study his fanny off." Well, he had. He had made the sacrifices. The long nights studying, while others caught the Monday Night Football games, "House" reruns, and Saturday Night Live skits. Dinners were always on the run, generally out of a cardboard box or neatly folded wax paper. Yes, I'll take fries with that.

Medical school had been all Vranian had known for so long, and it was now time to take the next step, and arguably the biggest step. And it came down to this exam; this one board exam that would determine if he would achieve his goal. For twenty-one straight years, Johns Hopkins has had the #1 program in the country for Internal Medicine, and Vranian wanted it. He wanted it bad.

Vranian stared at the cold, gray glowing computer screen in front of him. Man, he was nervous.

Carefully he pulled two newly sharpened pencils from his shirt pocket and placed them toward the right edge of the desk, next to the scratch paper provided. Then he fished out the calculator from the same shirt pocket and placed it on the desk to his left. Finally, he took off his wristwatch and folded the linked metal band in such a way that he could form a little stand, and the face of the watch was angled up toward him so he could see the dial at all times. Knowing the time was crucial, especially as it got toward the end of the exam. Wasn't that the way many things in life worked out? Crunch time is at the end.

Vranian looked around the room. He could see heads and shoulders of the other students scurrying to get to their assigned computer stations. Time was drawing near.

He looked back down at the configuration of his desk—pencils to the right, calculator to the left, watch at the top. As he pondered the formation, a picture slowly developed in front him. It was a picture of a baseball field. It was the view that he had seen many times before, starting with his Little League days and straight on through his days on his high school team.

As catcher, he would peer out toward the mound, where Justin Verlander was when he fired those fastballs. On his right, an imaginary white chalk line angled its way off to first base--toward the pencils! The watch was on second, just past the pitcher's mound. And on third sat the calculator, cheating ever so slightly off the bag, ready to race home.

Vranian's heart settled a bit. He had been here before. The feelings he had—the nervousness, the anxiety of the situation, the pressure to perform—he had felt them all before.

***

He had never experienced anything like this. The crowds in the stands were so loud, yet he couldn't hear a thing. Vranian was thirteen years old and standing in the on-deck circle at the AAU Regional Championship game against the Virginia Beach Blasters. The winner of this game would go to the National Championships in Chickasha, Oklahoma. This was huge.

Derrick Mitchell, the cleanup batter, was walking to the plate. There was only one out, and two men were already on base. The Virginia Beach Blasters' coach was motioning for the outfield to pull in close, hoping to give his players a chance to fire the ball home in the event of a play at the plate.

Vranian rubbed the palm of his left hand. Playing catcher was tough, especially when Verlander was on the mound. Those fastballs hurt, even with the extra padding. He grabbed a doughnut and slid the ringed weight over the handle of the bat so that it caught on the meat of the bat, about two-thirds of the way down the barrel. It was his custom to swing the bat around with the extra weight, so that by the time Derrick hit, struck out, or walked, Vranian would be warmed up and ready to hit.

But while time seemed to stand still on one hand, it raced way too fast on the other. For this was not going to be a usual at bat for Derrick. Vranian stopped in mid-swing when he realized that the Blasters were intentionally walking Derrick. Four quick pitches and Vranian would be up to bat. The pressure mounted with each pitch, and he wasn't even standing at the plate yet!

"Ball four!" yelled the umpire, and all eyes turned to the next kid up to bat, Michael Vranian. He was so nervous that he almost forgot to knock the doughnut off the bat, but with a few quick taps of the handle on the ground, the doughnut came off and rolled to the far side of the on-deck circle.

Vranian stepped into the batter's box and faced the pitcher on the mound. He looked like he was standing on a mountain. Words such as "crisp," "polished," and "well-trained" echoed through his head as he recalled how the coaches talked almost admiringly about the Blasters. They were a darn good team, as evidenced by their long string of National Championship appearances and they deserved the accolades.

"Strike one!" yelled the umpire.

Vranian didn't swing. Vranian didn't even move, even when the pitcher took his windup and fired another pitch...

"Ball one!" Thank goodness, thought Vranian, still locked in position at the plate with the bat firmly rooted to his shoulder.

The count was one and one, and Vranian stepped out of the box to get his bearings. Game is tied at 2-2 late in extra innings. Bases are loaded, and I know they want me to hit a ground ball so they can get a double play. If I do hit a fly ball, the outfield is playing in so tight that they can catch it and still peg the guy tagging up on third when he runs for the plate. Vranian was amazed that he could process all of this, because all he really wanted to do is throw up.

He stepped back into the box and lifted the bat off his shoulder, as if to signal to the pitcher that he meant business. Maybe the pitcher would be intimidated and throw the ball into the stands or something.

But what happened next was even better.

Vranian took a healthy swing and caught the ball pure and flush, sending the ball straight over the center fielder's head.

The man on third scored easily and before Vranian could reach second base his teammates came yelling and screaming out of the dugout, lifted him on their shoulders, and carried him off the field. He'd won the game!

***

Back at the medical board exam, Vranian reached for the mouse and gave it the initial click.

"You may begin," read the large words on the computer screen.

With authority Vranian clicked to the first question. "Batter up!"

Ben Verlander with dad, Richard, following The Virginia Commonwealth Games, 2009

"Ben" there, done that!
(siblings and such)

Ben is Justin's younger brother. And yes, he plays baseball.

The first thing you should know about Ben is that he, like his parents, often has to work at maintaining his own identity. Don't get us wrong, Ben embraces his brother's fame, and is inspired by his success. But being the brother, the inevitable comparisons are often the first thing that people ask about. Is Ben as good as Justin? Is he a pitcher? Will he go to the Major Leagues?

Like in most families, our sons are in many ways as different as day and night, and to make comparisons is an unfair exercise and at best very subjective. The only comparison we care about is their equal commitment to be good men and to each follow their passion.

To the parents of athletes with younger brothers or sisters in the same sport, our advice is to encourage them to make their own mark in their own time. Allow them to recognize that the path they walk may take a different route, or twist into new territory altogether! Let their route be of their choosing, and if it's unfamiliar, provide all of the support and encouragement you can and head down a new path together.

Every young person is special and has gifts that are unique to them. Our job as parents is to help them unlock their own potential and follow their own dreams.

As for comparisons…?

Both of our sons will always be All-Stars in our eyes!

Ben Verlander with
championship plaque
Myrtle Beach, S.C.
RBA Cardinals

Ben garnered All District and Team MVP honor while at Goochland High School. He accepted a scholarship offer to play baseball at Old Dominion University.

Ben graduates from
Goochland High School
with honors and a
proud mom.

Ben celebrates with brother Justin and Detroit manager, Jim Leyland in the Tigers clubhouse follo[wing] the ALCS Championship game at Comerica Park in 2006.

Practical Matters
(and other general advice)

"It's getting late early..."
Yogi Berra

Preparation is key
Get things ready the night before. Are uniforms washed? Do you know where hats, socks, belts, and other "elusive" items are? Don't wait till you walk out the door. Put your name and number in your hat. And make sure you have your stuff before you leave.

Be on time
If you are early you are on time; if you are on time you are late; if you are late you are forgotten. For parents, getting your youngster to practice on time today will help to assure consideration of others later on.

GPS makes you stupid
If there seems to be a better way to get somewhere, there probably is…. Try looking at a map if you have one.

Weather or not?
Plan for the worst, hope for the best, and don't believe the weatherman. When it comes to staying warm it's always easier to bring too many clothes than to wish you had brought more. Sleeping bags are great on those really cold days. On hot summer days always bring sunscreen and lots of water (hydrate the night before). Umbrellas should have a permanent place in your trunk. Ponchos are even better.

Get some sleep
Parents and athletes perform better with adequate rest.

Time management
Use your time wisely. Is it really that important to get that last stain completely out of that uniform? Don't you have better things to do?

Volunteer
Help the coaches, they can't carry everything… Be the scorekeeper; it's a great way to learn everyone's name and the coach will love you! Same holds true for concession duty.

Silence is golden
Watch what you say. You never know who is listening… It is often best to remain silent and be thought a fool than to open your mouth and remove all doubt. And try not to embarrass your kids. Let the coach do the coaching. Who you are and what you do speak much more loudly than what you say.

Take care of the little things and the big things will take care of themselves…

Your Money, Your Time, Your Future

"There's a sucker born every minute."
P.T. Barnum

Spend Wisely (out of town trips, camps, etc.)

Going out of town does not make you a better baseball player. Trips together are nice, but the quality of the competition and the coaching is more important than the location of the tournament. Likewise, an invitation to a camp does not make you a prospect or guarantee you anything. The better camps do offer excellent instruction in a group setting and present some opportunities to get noticed. Others are just moneymakers. Do your research and attend those where coaches from schools or teams that you want to play for are either hosts or in attendance. Pro-style MLB tryouts are usually open to all—and free. Don't expect to walk away on the 25 man roster, but you may get yourself on a prospect list or the recruiting list for a good college program. Pro scouts and college recruiters do network with one another.

Individual Instruction

If you can afford it, there is nothing better than one-on-one instruction with a good teacher. To save expense, try splitting an hour a week with another player. As young athletes progress they can often earn money for lessons by passing along what they have learned to younger players. Or, if you have to choose between keeping last years bat and eight weeks worth of one on one instruction, go with the coaching.

The $500 bat can wait…

College or Pro?

If your young athlete is being scouted by MLB and is considering signing a pro contract and foregoing college, there are several important things to consider. Obviously the talent is there, or they wouldn't be in the position of even having to think about it… Some pro scouts put a lot of pressure on a youngster to sign and turn pro out of high school. As parents, we need to educate ourselves and our student athlete on the bigger picture before deciding. One thing that should be taken into account is the instant leap from "high school kid" to adult. Can your youngster handle leaving home with a little money and heading off to play ball in the Minor Leagues? Are they emotionally mature enough to enter an adult world, away from home, and all that entails? For most youngsters, college life is a nice transition to adulthood and a bond remains between parents and their sons and daughters in an academic setting that fosters independence and maturity, yet still has rules, parameters and standards within a structured environment. And if the goal is to play in the Major Leagues, here is an important point that most scouts don't mention: on average, whether a prospect signs a pro contract after high school or goes to college, the years spent in the Minor Leagues prior to arrival at the Major League level will amount to about the same time necessary to attend college and get a degree! And that is for those few that are good enough to make it to the Major Leagues at all!

Please take the time to talk to players and their families that have been down this road for guidance.

Agents, Advisors, and Financial Consultants

Top prospects can expect an onslaught of interest in personal representation, and the higher the potential, the more folks that will come calling. With high profile amateurs nearing the draft, this can become very intense and often overwhelming. It can be a very useful exercise for parents to act as a buffer to filter through the many offers to represent a prospective young client with a bright future. Do your homework, trim the list down to a few reputable firms, and then help your athlete with the decision making process. Schools, and coaches can partner with the family of these student athletes to help insulate them and allow them to focus on their sport and their school life until the time comes to make these decisions.

Remember that college or high school athletes can not hire an agent or accept anything of monetary value from individuals that offer such services prior to the draft. There are provisions for "advisors" that comply with NCAA regulations, and most reputable agents understand compliance issues, but don't leave your amateur eligibility to chance! Know the rules!

Please take the time to talk to players and their families that have been down this road for guidance.

"He ain't heavy, he's my brother."

The Hollies, 1969

Photo courtesy of the Goochland Gazette/Ken Odor.

Follow Your Heart
(family matters)

" We should not judge each day by the harvest that you reap, but by the seeds that you sow."

Robert Louis Stevenson

Kathy and I have been married for thirty-seven years. My parents were married fifty years before my mom passed away in 2004, and Kathy's parents were together until her father's passing in 1975, the year we were wed. They are truly the greatest generation and who we are today is due largely to them. We are our parent's legacy and our children become ours. Kathy and I never proclaim ourselves to be the best parents, but like our own parents we do know in our hearts that we have always done OUR best. Our opinions on raising children are just that—Our Opinion.

We have written this book based on years of experience, observation, and trial and error. This much we are sure about: we are truly blessed and we know it.

So What Do We Believe?

We believe in God.

We believe in family.

We believe that the only way to do great work is to love what you do.

We believe in character.

We believe in having supper as a family.

We believe in dogs.

We believe in kindness.

We believe kids should have a bedtime.

We believe co-ed sleepovers are a bad idea.

We believe being good parents isn't always popular.

We believe in baseball.

We believe that your reputation is what you are perceived to be. Your character is what you are.

We believe in following our instincts.

In the early 90's we moved to Goochland Virginia, a rural community, looking for a simpler life. People criticized us. They said Justin would be better served in an elite baseball district and would never get noticed at a small country school. We still moved… It just felt right.

In 2000 my job required me to move to Maryland. We decided not to move our kids. I lived with a friend for awhile, only coming home on weekends. I worked really hard, but being away from my family so much was killing me. After a year, we decided I should try to go back to my old job at the phone company and come back home. A lot less money, but it just felt right. Ultimately, my boss and my friend, Peter Catucci, who later passed away, allowed me to work from an office near our home. The last words I heard him speak before his untimely death were, "practice love." I'll never forget him; or his words.

Later in 2000, after coming back home to work, Kathy decided it was time to forego the corporate world and be a stay-at-home mom. Even though times were tough, we decided to do it because it was the right thing to do.

In 2004 we helped Justin make a decision to go to college, which for all practical purposes took him out of the MLB draft. It felt like the right thing to do.

Justin (and later Ben) accepted a scholarship to play baseball at Old Dominion University for then head coach Tony Guzzo. We were criticized for not going to a "big name" program. You see, this man told us he would take care of our son, and we believed him. It felt right.

In 2011, I was forced by my employer to pick between my job, and taking proper care of my dad. With my late friend's words, "practice love" as my guide, I quit my job. It felt like the right thing to do.

Later that spring we began talking to parents and kids about baseball, and life. People said we should write a book. A new journey began. It just feels right.

Do what feels right when it comes to raising your children.

Your conscience may be God speaking to you...

Family Relay

I have stressed that building skills is hard work, and well, it is. But your kids don't have to know that! Make it fun. Kids are much more likely to stick with it if they are having fun. And don't overlook that building skills can be a family activity as well.

For example, a friend of mine told me about how he would search all over the city to find a ballpark that was smaller than the ballparks his son was playing on. He would then take a bucket of balls and let his son smash ball after ball over the fence. It was a huge confidence builder, but the son got the biggest kick when his dad would scramble over the fence to retrieve all those balls!

Another father told me about how he drilled a hole through the diameter of a baseball and then fed a cord through the hole. He'd tie a knot in one end of the cord to keep the ball from sliding off, and then he'd take the cord and swing it around and around over his head in a wide circle so that his son could take swings at the "pitches." They'd stand out in the yard for hours swinging at the ball attached to that cord, hitting homer after homer, and the dad's arm didn't get so tired.

One of our family's favorite skill-honing techniques involved going over to the high school and doing some drills. Goochland High School, like many other small schools, had only one large field and both the football gridiron and baseball diamond were carved out of it. To the baseball player, it looked like you were sliding into the 40 yard line. I guess it could be confusing, but we managed pretty well.

In the off-season, Justin would keep his arm strength up by throwing baseballs the length of the football field. He'd stand on one end of the field and hurl balls 100 yards or more from one end zone to the other. He'd get pretty tired and bored walking the length of the field to gather all the tossed balls, so we decided to turn it into a family event.

Justin would stand in the far end zone and throw the ball the length of the field to me in the opposite end zone. I'd take the ball and toss it to Kathy on about the fifty yard line or so. Kathy would then throw the ball to Ben, standing around Justin's twenty yard line, and then Ben would toss the ball back to Justin. Justin would give it another heave and we'd all go through the same routine again.

The family relay!

Kathy with parents Olympia and Minton Ryder
2/1/1975

Myrtle Beach vacation 1992

San Francisco Trip 1991

Justin at Cub Scout Pizza Day!
1989

Dad with the boys

Justin and Barney our Beagle

Justin with fellow 7 year old Kevin
Marshall, Tuckahoe Little League Royals

Justin with Barney and Zach

Niece Emelia in a tree

Our niece Camille's Sunday best!

Grandma with Ben

Grandparents and Ben on Graduation Day

Ryder family

Riley

Ben Justin and Barney "smoochfest! "

Our nephew William Ryder

" top of the world"

"Uncle" Lewis

Justin with cousins Aly and Katy

"whad I say?"

Justin and Grandma Ryde

Our nieces, Aly, Katy, and Co.

Our sister-in-law Denise and "Miss B"

Grandma Verlander and Pop

Cleveland 7/4/2005

Whetstone Story

Several years ago a representative of a Major League Baseball team was in town doing some background checks on Justin. For lack of a better way of putting it, he was looking for character witnesses. For good reason, professional teams are reluctant to spend money on faulty goods. Bad character equals bad investment. And draft day was right around the corner.

Who did this representative visit?

Our old neighbor, Gene Whetstone.

And what did Gene Whetstone say?

Gene Whetstone and his wife, Dee, said one of the nicest things that a parent can ever hear:

"Sir," he said to the representative, "we don't have any children, but if we did, we'd want them to be just like Justin and Ben."

Justin was the first pick for the Detroit Tigers that season.

"Life is a bobsled track. You've got to let the child go down the hill, but it's up to the parents to create the walls that keep him from flying off into the crowd."

– Michael Vranian, M.D., catcher on Justin's AAU baseball team